SMOOTHIE BOWLS

50 Healthy Smoothie Bowl Recipes

Sarah Spencer

Copyrights

All rights reserved © Sarah Spencer and The Cookbook Publisher. No part of this publication or the information in it may be quoted from or reproduced in any form by means such as printing, scanning, photocopying, or otherwise without prior written permission of the copyright holder.

Disclaimer and Terms of Use

Effort has been made to ensure that the information in this book is accurate and complete. However, the author and the publisher do not warrant the accuracy of the information, text, and graphics contained within the book due to the rapidly changing nature of science, research, known and unknown facts, and internet. The author and the publisher do not hold any responsibility for errors, omissions, or contrary interpretation of the subject matter herein. This book is presented solely for motivational and informational purposes only.

The recipes provided in this book are for informational purposes only and are not intended to provide dietary advice. A medical practitioner should be consulted before making any changes in diet. Additionally, recipe cooking times may require adjustment depending on age and quality of appliances. Readers are strongly urged to take all precautions to ensure ingredients are fully cooked in order to avoid the dangers of foodborne illnesses. The recipes and suggestions provided in this book are solely the opinion of the author. The author and publisher do not take any responsibility for any consequences that may result due to following the instructions provided in this book.

ISBN: 978-1981187836

Printed in the United States

Contents

Introduction 1
   What Is A "Smoothie In A Bowl"? 2
   Smoothie Ingredients.. 3
   Preening Up Your Smoothie Bowl 7
Smoothie Bowl Recipes 11
   Chocolate Peanut Butter Smoothie Bowl 11
   Fruity Crunch Smoothie Bowl 12
   Blueberry Delight Smoothie Bowl 13
   Coconut and Banana Oats Smoothie Bowl 15
   Pitaya Breakfast Smoothie Bowl 17
   Strawberry Acai Bowl 18
   Creamy Coconut and Avocado Smoothie Bowl 19
   Blueberry Banana Bonanza Bowl 21
   Pumpkin Pie Smoothie Bowl 22
   Green Matcha Mint Smoothie Bowl 23
   Blueberry Buckwheat Smoothie Bowl 25
   Pumpkin Papaya Acai Breakfast Bowl 26
   Super Green Smoothie Bowl 27
   Turmeric Avocado Banana Smoothie Bowl 29
   Raspberry Mango Smoothie Bowl 30
   Avocado Persimmon Breakfast Bowl 31
   Raspberry Melon Baobab Smoothie 32
   Carrot Cake Smoothie Bowl 33
   Mango Lucama Super-Green Smoothie 35
   Chocolate Hazelnut Hemp Smoothie Bowl 36
   Pineapple, Banana, and Peach Smoothie Bowl 37
   Berry Smoothie Bowl with Peach and Orange 38
   Blueberry, Spinach, Pineapple Smoothie Bowl 39
   Peaches and Cream Smoothie Bowl 40
   Dark Cherry Smoothie Bowl 41
   Blueberry Cacao Smoothie Bowl 42
   Blue Morning Smoothie Bowl 43

Sunrise Smoothie Bowl 44
Chocolate Almond Butter Smoothie Bowl 45
Pina-Colada Breakfast Smoothie 46
Choco Cherry Breakfast Smoothie Bowl 47
Blueberry Cheesecake Smoothie Bowl..............................48
Vegan Blackberry Coconut Smoothie 49
Banana Cream Pie Smoothie Bowl....................................50
Mango, Beet and Banana Smoothie Bowl..........................51
Vanilla Raspberry Smoothie..52
Strawberry Cheesecake Smoothie Bowl............................53
Mango Ginger Good-Eats Bowl 54
Peanut Butter Berry Acai Bowl 55
Chocolate-Mint Green Smoothie Bowl 56
Enlighten Smoothie Bowl 57
Muesli Greek Yogurt Smoothie Bowl 58
Cherry Berry Smoothie Bowl 59
Chai Infused Chia Smoothie Bowl 60
Cherry Apple Smoothie Fare 61
Banana Split Smoothie Bowl..62
Grapefruit Smoothie Bowl 63
Chocolate Tahini Dates Smoothie Bowl.............................64
Butternut Molasses Smoothie Bowl 65
Probiotic Kefir Smoothie Bowl...67
Vanilla Almond Smoothie Bowl 68
More Books by Sarah Spencer 69
Appendix - Cooking Conversion Charts................................71

Introduction

If your mornings are drab and your breakfast is dull, just a mindless routine, you need to revamp your table spread. As everybody is aware of the virtues of this first meal, people look for creative ways to incorporate nourishment to the breakfast table, leading to the newest fad: Smoothie Bowls!

People are increasingly looking for healthier breakfast options instead of the grease drenched fares of cholesterol and gluten-ridden plates of nightmare. If you peruse the Instagram feed of any creative health fanatic, you'll stumble across buckwheat porridges and chia pudding shots, along with its more contemporary, and dare I say gorgeous cousin, the smoothie bowls.

Seamlessly integrating the fruity goodness of a smoothie with the dig-in appeal of a breakfast bowl, the smoothie bowl is a recent phenomenon, and everybody is rushing to jump on the bandwagon. Blogs and webpages on the internet are brimming with delectable trends, each marking their own spin on the breakfast spread.

The smoothie fad, however, struck me as a bit out of the blue and it took me a while to absorb the contemporary philosophy. The main reservation stemmed from the fear of a drinkable breakfast and feeling famished a few hours down the road. However, delving deep in to the ideology of smoothie in a bowl, I have unearthed my idyllic breakfast!

What Is A "Smoothie In A Bowl"?

Smoothies are synonymous with slurping a heavenly concoction out of a glass where mixing fruits, vegetables and other ingredients becomes an art. However, nothing could be a more glorious start to a day than a hearty bowl of scrumptious breakfast smoothie! Yes, it is what it says: smoothie is a bowl.

The luscious creamy texture of the smoothie, incorporating all the goodness nature has to offer, contrasted by the nutty, crunchy layer of toppings, makes this fare almost a luxury! These energy-boosting recipes tantalize your taste buds and make your body swoon in gratitude.

Generally, the texture of the smoothie bowl is thickly creamy, akin to a pudding; but it can be slightly liquid too. A drinkable smoothie is a mixture of equal parts liquid and solid ingredients, whereas, for a smoothie in a bowl, the liquids are reduced to half. In addition, instead of adding ice, which could water down the blend, a frozen banana or frozen berries are usually employed.

Great for breakfast, post workout snack, a quick lunch, or dessert, they are a delicious, satisfying, and nutritious twist on cereal. Consider it a complete nutrient-dense makeover of good old cereal and milk! The fact the breakfast is liquid goes to redeem it further by helping the body assimilate it faster and it is essentially indispensable for busy bees. Enjoy these delectable smoothie recipes to revitalize your body, amp up your energy levels and start your day, sunny side up!

Smoothie Ingredients

Five minutes to breakfast? Anyone can be a culinary Picasso with a smoothie bowl. The combinations you fabricate are limited only by your imagination (well, that and whatever happens to be in your fridge and pantry). Banish the dreaded boring breakfast, as these exciting and festive surprise packages of goodness make waking up a little easier each morning.

Always listen to your body in the morning? What are you in the mood for? If you think you need a little more fuel for your day, toss a half-cup of all-natural granola or trail mix into your smoothie. You can also top it with sliced fruit, honey or agave, hemp seeds, coconut shreds, dried fruit, and nuts. Craving indulgence? What could go wrong with adding peanut butter and dark chocolate chips to your breakfast! The possibilities are endless.

Choose at least one victual from each category, whip out your blender and let your creativity run wild!

- **Greens and Other Veggies**: Romaine, spinach, cucumber, kale greens, and celery

- **Frozen or Fresh Fruits:** Pears, pineapple, oranges, peaches, acai, mango, dates, raspberries, figs, blueberries, bananas, kiwis, papaya, lemons, apples, limes, grapefruit, blood oranges, strawberries, plums, etc.

Tip: When freezing fruits, the right way is to peel first and then store the slices or chunks in a zip lock bag for easy handling!

- **Proteins**: Plant-based protein powders (brown rice, pea, Sunwarrior, Vega, organic grass-fed whey protein, etc.), chia seeds, hemp seeds, nut butters, etc.

- **Healthy Fats:** Coconut oil, chia seeds, hemp seeds, avocados, and any other nuts and seeds you have on hand!

- **Super foods**: Matcha tea powder, avocados, spirulina, bee pollen, nut milks, maca powder, lucama, raw gluten-free oats, cocoa nibs, chlorella, sprouted buckwheat groats, hemp seeds, cinnamon, cayenne, young coconut meat, unsweetened shredded coconut, coconut water, chia seeds, etc.

- **Ice** to thicken your smoothie and add texture.

- **Liquid**: Unsweetened almond or other milks, coconut water, filtered water, etc.

- **Optional Sweetener**: If your smoothie base needs a little additional sweetness, agave is a great way to add it if you are watching your carbohydrate intake. Otherwise, any sweetener you might add to a normal smoothie would work in the smoothie bowl as well, but it is a good to opt for natural sweeteners.

Play around with flavors, pile on your toppings, grab a spoon and dive in!

Note:

As a smoothie bowl personifies all that is fresh and vigorous in our world, it should not be contaminated with preservative-ridden or unhealthy ingredients. Aspire to use natural sweeteners, such as raw honey, real maple syrup or organic coconut palm sugar to get the most nutrients out of these recipes. It is prudent to avoid using cow's milk, and substitute different types of dairy-free milks, like coconut milk, almond milk, or organic grass-fed goat milk or cheese. You can also opt for table salt instead of sea salt, low-fat Greek yogurt for regular yogurt, and replace canola and vegetable oil with coconut oil, olive oil or ghee. Buy fruits that are in season, and if possible, organic. When shopping for groceries, be a label sleuth. Compare brands by the nutrition facts label.

Preparing Nuts and Oats

To make your smoothies thicker and creamier, how you prepare the base makes all the difference. As oats make up, for the most part, a choice ingredient, they have to be soaked overnight to render them blend-able. This way, they break down easily in the blender along with other ingredients, and you won't have any stray chunks floating on the top!

The same could be said for nuts, not the ones for toppings, but the nuts going in to the smoothie. It is a good idea to let them soak the entire night, preferably in milk (you could use the same milk for your smoothie), so they'll be ready in the morning!

Dried dates can also add thickness and a caramel-like sweetness, but be sure to pit them first. If they feel hard, soak them in hot water until they soften, then drain, reserving the liquid, and pat dry. The liquid can be used to dilute and sweeten your smoothie bowl.

Preening Up Your Smoothie Bowl

A smoothie doesn't just make a delectable breakfast option, but a glorious sight to behold. To incorporate texture and a chewy dimension to your smoothie, and to simulate the oh-so-pretty bowls Instagrammers rave about, toppings are an essential element. Just like the icing on top of the cake! Even if you make the same smoothie bowl day after day, garnishing it creatively and with a plethora of toppings makes all the difference!

Some commendable topping ideas include homemade (or store bought) granola, seeds, nuts and nut butters, fresh fruits, dried fruits, oats, cinnamon, flaxseeds, chocolate chunks, pepitas, sunflower seeds, pecans, hazelnuts, macadamia nuts, pistachios, dollops of coconut cream, a drizzle of coconut oil or a hearty smattering of lovely, colorful berries.

The choices are endless! You can even incorporate your favorite supplement powder, such as vanilla protein or vegan, to imbue an additional nutritional kick and jumpstart your metabolism to see you through the day! To enhance the protein content of the smoothies, silken tofu can be added, or slivers of toasted almonds or roasted soy nuts. As I use granola as my favorite topping in almost all recipes, here's how you can make your own granola bars and eat organic!

Homemade Granola Bars Recipe

Ingredients
- 3 tablespoons light brown sugar
- 3 cups rolled oats
- ½ teaspoon ground cinnamon
- ½ teaspoon salt
- 1/3 cup honey
- ¼ cup coconut oil (Heat to liquefy)
- Few drops of Vanilla extract
- Dried fruits and chopped nuts, to taste

Preparation

1. Preheat oven to 300ºF.
2. In a large bowl, combine the flour, rolled oats, sugar, and cinnamon and stir to combine. Set aside.
3. In another bowl, toss together honey, coconut oil and vanilla extract and pour over the oats mixture.
4. Combine thoroughly until the oats are completely coated.
5. Spread the mixture evenly over a thin prepared baking sheet and bake for 15 minutes.
6. Stir lightly and toss back in the oven until the oats attain a slightly golden hue.
7. Place the baking sheet over a wire rack to cool. Sprinkle dried fruits, chopped nuts and seeds as desired.

Smoothie Bowl Recipes

Chocolate Peanut Butter Smoothie Bowl

This thick delectable chocolate smoothie bowl would make a drool-worthy breakfast for the entire family. There are a plethora of toppings which can be thrown in to impart a crunchy freshness to the scrumptious bowl, such as fresh fruits, dried fruits, nuts, seeds, chocolate, or peanut butter.

Serves 2

Ingredients
Smoothie
8 pitted dates
½ cup rice milk
4 medium bananas (It's good to freeze them beforehand)
8 tablespoons unsweetened cocoa powder or carob powder
2 tablespoons crunchy organic peanut butter

Toppings
1 banana, sliced
1 tablespoon shredded coconut
1 tablespoon chocolate chips
1 tablespoon crushed peanuts
1 tablespoon sesame seeds

Preparation
1. Blend all the smoothie ingredients together until a smooth consistency is reached. If your blender is not powerful enough, you can avoid freezing the bananas, or chop them into small chunks before putting in.
2. Add heaps of your favorite toppings and dive in! Making breakfast has never been so easy.

Nutrition Facts per serving
Calories 829, carbs 177g, fats 21g, proteins 16g,
sodium 92 mg, sugars 112g,.

Fruity Crunch Smoothie Bowl

If you are looking for a way to make mornings bearable, this hearty delectable smoothie brings a hallelujah from your lips! The scrumptious blend of berries, kale, bananas, chia seeds, and almond is beautifully creative and incorporated with the creamy texture of yogurt, makes an irresistible breakfast.

Serves 3

Ingredients

Smoothie
1 cup chopped kale
1 tablespoon chia seeds
1 cup unsweetened almond milk
1 ½ cups mixed berries, preferably frozen
1 small banana, frozen
1-2 tablespoons agave

Toppings
3 strawberries
1 tablespoon coconut shavings
1 granola bar, crumbled (p8 for the recipe)
1 tablespoon blueberries

Preparation
1. Blend kale with almond milk and chia seeds, until a smooth puree forms.
2. Add the berries and bananas, taking pains to leave a little texture.
3. Pour the smoothie into a bowl and top with the scrumptious topping ingredients. Be creative with the presentation!

Nutrition facts per serving
Calories 505, carbs 99g, fats 10g, proteins 6g,
sodium 278mg, sugars 63g.

Blueberry Delight Smoothie Bowl

This thick, richly creamy smoothie bowl is reminiscent of a beloved berry-infused ice cream, only much healthier and packed with nutrients. The base, prepared with blueberries and raw honey, packs an antioxidant and anti-inflammatory punch to revamp your energy levels, being the super foods they are. Blueberries are also rich in manganese, which helps convert the body's intake of proteins, carbohydrates, and fats into energy.

Serves 3

Ingredients
Smoothie
2 cups blueberries
1 cup unsweetened almond milk
1 banana
1 tablespoon raw honey
1 teaspoon vanilla extract
1 ½ cups oats, (soaked overnight)

Toppings
1 tablespoon chopped goji berries
1 tablespoon cacao nibs
2 tablespoons slivered almonds
1 teaspoon chia speed
1 teaspoon toasted coconut (shredded)

Preparation
1. Toss in all the smoothie ingredients in to the blender and mix at medium speed.
2. Pour out when an ice cream consistency is reached.
3. Sprinkle the toppings generously and indulge in your sweet tooth with this heartily satisfying (but not too heavy) smoothie!

Nutrition Facts Per serving
Calories 1257, carbs 235g, fats 20g, proteins 44g, sodium 190 mg, sugars 56g.

Coconut and Banana Oats Smoothie Bowl

If you can't escape to the tropics, bring the tropics to your table. This refreshingly healthy recipe, with the wonderful combination of coconut and banana, will greatly revitalize your mornings and enable you to take the day in your stride. The baked quinoa cereal incorporates a nice creamy texture to the base, while the crunchy, fiber-rich oats curbs your carb cravings for hours on end! The sprig of mint on top brings that much needed spring goodness!

Serves 2

Ingredients
For Coconut Banana Smoothie
1/3 cup rolled oats
1 cup coconut milk
1 tablespoon chia seeds
Pinch of Salt
1 banana
Few drops of vanilla essence

For the Black Sesame Quinoa Cereal
1 cup almonds, roughly chopped
½ cup cashews, roughly chopped
¼ cup flax seeds
½ cup black sesame seeds
3 ¼ cups cooked quinoa
2 tablespoons honey
A few drops of vanilla extract
Pinch of salt
¼ cup coconut oil, melted

Toppings
½ mango, chopped
Sprig of mint
1 tablespoon chopped chocolate chunks
Coconut butter (to taste)

Preparation

For Black Sesame Quinoa Cereal
1. Line two baking sheets with parchment.
2. Stir all ingredients for the black sesame quinoa cereal together and spread over the prepared baking sheets.
3. Bake for 35 minutes, at 350°F, stirring occasionally, until a light golden hue is achieved.
4. Allow to cool down at room temperature.

For the Coconut Banana Oats
1. Mix all ingredients for the coconut banana oats together, sparing half the coconut milk, and refrigerate overnight.
2. Toss in to the blender in the morning, along with the remaining coconut milk and blend at medium speed, until a creamy consistency is reached.
3. Pour the oats smoothie in to a bowl.
4. Top it off with a sprinkling of crunchy black sesame quinoa cereal, and the remaining toppings. Enjoy!

Nutrition facts per serving
Calories 900, carbs 119g, fats 36g, proteins 27g, sodium 144mg, sugars 16g.

Pitaya Breakfast Smoothie Bowl

The slightly sweet pitaya, or dragon fruit, is a rich source of antioxidants, magnesium, fiber, active enzymes and vitamins A, B and C — which support a healthy immune system, refurbish the body's energy pool after strenuous workout, and aid with digestion. Not to mention, the fiercely pink color of the concoction makes it almost too pretty to eat!

Serves 1-2

Ingredients
Smoothie
1 cup frozen pitaya puree
1-2 bananas
½ cup frozen berries
½ cup almond milk
2 tablespoons vegetable protein powder

Toppings
1 tablespoon hemp hearts
1 tablespoon bee pollen
2 tablespoons goji berries

Preparation
1. Blend all smoothie ingredients together at medium speed, until a smooth puree forms.
2. Top with the delectable topping options and enjoy the scrumptious fare!

Nutrition facts per serving
Calories 333, carbs 55g, fats 6g, proteins 20g, sodium 391mg, sugars 27g.

Strawberry Acai Bowl

If the summer heat is draining your vitality, this chia-infused concoction with dark purple acai berries will supply your body with energy revving carbohydrates, and anti-oxidant packed nutrients. Deemed by the Brazilians as the "Beauty Berry," acai berries truly do the body good from inside out, giving you revamped energy levels, enhanced metabolism, gorgeous skin, lustrous hair and a boosted immune system. There's a reason these berries are famous!

Serves 2

Ingredients
Smoothie
1 medium banana, frozen
¾ cups raspberries, frozen
½ cups blueberries
1 teaspoon acai berry powder
1 scoop vanilla protein powder
1 cup water
1 teaspoon chia seeds

Toppings
1 tablespoon shredded coconuts
1 granola bar, crumbled
2 tablespoons mixed berries

Preparation
1. Toss all smoothie ingredients except chia seeds into the blender and puree until smooth.
2. Stir in chia seeds and allow the mixture to sit for a few minutes. The seeds absorb water and thicken the consistency of the smoothie bowl.
3. Blend again and pour into a bowl.
4. Top with the hearty toppings for a delectable breakfast!

Nutrition facts per serving
Calories 348, carbs 58g, fats 6g, proteins 24g,
sodium 325mg, sugars 30g.

Creamy Coconut and Avocado Smoothie Bowl

This gorgeous enough to win the Miss-America-for-Food Pageant smoothie is simply glorious and revitalizing. Although many might associate avocado with savory foods, this stealthy ingredient is insanely fulfilling and gives a delectable flavor to the smoothie in a bowl!

Serves 3

Ingredients
Smoothie
½ cup cashews
6 tablespoons low fat coconut milk
¼ cup mashed avocado
¾ cup unsweetened almond milk
2 tablespoons vanilla protein powder
¼ cup chopped kale
1 frozen banana
¼ cup vanilla Greek yogurt

Toppings
1 tablespoon coconut shavings
1 tablespoon pomegranate seeds
1 tablespoon cashews

Preparation
1. Preheat the oven to 400°F.
2. Line a baking sheet with parchment and roast the cashews for 35 minutes.
3. Once the roasted cashews are cooled, soak them in water and leave overnight.

4. Drain the water in the morning and blend the cashews with coconut milk, and a pinch of salt, until a creamy paste forms. Set aside.
5. Blend the rest of the smoothie ingredients until a smooth consistency is achieved, and pour in a bowl.
6. Swirl some Cashew Cream over the top, sprinkle the heartwarming toppings and devour right away!

Nutrition fact per serving
Calories 333, carbs 55g, fats 6g, proteins 20g, sodium 391mg, sugars 27g.

Blueberry Banana Bonanza Bowl

What could be more sumptuous than combining two astounding fruits in to one nutrient-dense bowl of goodness? Laden with antioxidant rich berries, vitamin C, K, manganese, proteins, and healthy fats, then topped with a sweet crunch to indulge your sweet tooth, this bowl truly fulfils the childhood wish of wolfing down ice cream for breakfast — it's just way more healthy.

Serves 2

Recipe
Smoothie
3 cups fresh spinach
1 banana, frozen
1 cup blueberries, frozen
½ cup almond milk
1 scoop vanilla protein powder
1 tablespoon Organic Almond Butter (Melted)
1 teaspoon maca powder
1 pinch cinnamon
Ice

Toppings
1 Granola bar, crumbled

Preparation
1. Combine all smoothie ingredients in a blender and blend at high speed until a thick puree forms.
2. Pour in a bowl, top with the crumbles of your favorite granola bar, and dive in!

Nutrition facts per serving
Calories 390, carbs 55g, fats 12g, proteins 24g, sodium 174mg, sugars 24g.

Pumpkin Pie Smoothie Bowl

Want to ditch the guilt and devour the Grande pumpkin pie with flair? While Pumpkin Spice Lattes from Starbucks can do damage to the waistline, this healthy rendition not only lets you indulge in your cravings but supplies a burst of nutrition. Abundant in vitamin B complex, vitamins C, E, A, and minerals such as calcium, phosphorus and potassium, this concoction gives you lasting energy.

Serves 1-2

Ingredients
Smoothie
½ cup low-fat plain yogurt
1 cup milk
1 cup pumpkin puree
1 banana
1 tablespoon chia seeds
1 pinch ground ginger
1 pinch ground cinnamon
1 pinch ground cloves
1 pinch salt

Toppings
1 tablespoon shredded coconut
1 granola bar, crumbled
2 whole wheat crackers, crumbled

Preparation
1. Combine all smoothie ingredients in a blender, and pulse until smooth.
2. Pour into a bowl and sprinkle the toppings and a dollop of coconut cream on top, and dig in to the big bowl of heaven.

Nutrition facts per serving
Calories 486, carbs 77g, fats 14g, proteins 21g, sodium 211mg, sugars 48g.

Green Matcha Mint Smoothie Bowl

Want an insane caffeine buzz without the crash and jitters? Matcha is your savior. Matcha is widely believed to boost metabolism, energy, and concentration, and calm the body and mind. Reap the innumerable goodness of these antioxidant-packed Japanese tea leaves (rich in fiber, chlorophyll, and vitamins) by whipping up this delicious smoothie and top it off with crunchy, delicious, super-power ingredients to go an extra mile.

Serves 2-3

Ingredients

Smoothie
1/3 cup soaked raw cashews
3 cups loose-packed greens
3 bananas, frozen
3 sprigs of mint Leaves
3 teaspoon matcha powder
1 teaspoon vanilla powder
2 scoops vanilla protein powder
3 ½ cups unsweetened almond milk
1 tablespoon cacao nibs
Maple syrup, to taste

Toppings
1 tablespoon coconut flakes
1 tablespoon hemp seeds or sesame seeds
1 tablespoon cacao nibs
2 tablespoons puffed quinoa
Few sprigs of mint

Preparation

1. In an upright blender, blend all smoothie ingredients except cacao nibs, until a smooth consistency is achieved.
2. Toss the cacao nibs in the blender and pulse to break them up.
3. Pour into a bowl and shake up the smoothie with some of the topping assortments, and top it off with a dollop of whipped coconut cream.

Nutrition facts per serving

Calories 32, carbs 77g, fats 10g, proteins 12g, sodium 190mg, sugars 18g.

Blueberry Buckwheat Smoothie Bowl

For those avoiding gluten, this decadently creamy pudding bowl has no cereal grains, yet it packs bundles of hearty wholeness in every bite. Contrary to common belief, buckwheat is not a cereal grain but a fruit seed, rich in magnesium, fiber, proteins, copper and manganese, and renowned for lowering cholesterol, blood sugar levels, and blood pressure, making it a far superior alternative!

Serves 2-3

Ingredients
Smoothie
1 cup buckwheat groats
2 cups blueberries
2 tablespoons maple syrup
½ cup milk
1 banana
1 teaspoon vanilla extract
Juice of half a lemon

Preparation
1. Soak buckwheat groats in water overnight and drain well in the morning.
2. Blend blueberries with maple syrup until a smooth puree forms.
3. Reserve half of this sauce and toss in the rest of the smoothie ingredients in the blender, until creamy.
4. Pour in a bowl, drizzle the remaining blueberry puree for a marbled effect and top with fresh fruits, as pleases your palette.

Nutrition facts per serving
Calories 236, carbs 54g, fats 3g, proteins 6g,
sodium 2.5mg, sugars 18g.

Pumpkin Papaya Acai Breakfast Bowl

Brazilians rave about their beautiful people, pristine beaches, and the berry that-is-worthy-of-crowning-the-beauty-pageant. If you have not incorporated this superfood into your diet yet, you are missing out on an extreme powerhouse. This berry has been heralded for its incalculable health benefits, and supplemented with the delectable taste of beloved pumpkin, it makes waking up a lot easier.

Serves 2-3

Ingredients
Smoothie
½ can organic pumpkin puree
½ cup papaya
1 frozen unsweetened acai smoothie pack
1 ripe banana
1 tablespoon maca powder
1 tablespoon cinnamon and pumpkin spice
1 cup almond milk

Toppings
1 tablespoon goji berries
1 tablespoon pomegranate seeds
1 banana, sliced
2 tablespoons cashews, roasted

Preparation
1. Toss all smoothie ingredients in the blender and whip on high, until a smooth puree forms.
2. Top with your favorite crumbled granola bars, and turn your bowl in to a masterpiece with the rest of the topping ingredients.

Nutrition facts per serving
Calories 327, carbs 20g, fats 28g, proteins 4g,
sodium 21mg, and, sugars 11.6g

Super Green Smoothie Bowl

People might expect that smoothie bowls made with veggies taste would like freshly mowed lawns, but in fact the delectable ingredients incorporated in this smoothie mask the underlying veggie flavor so much, you wouldn't even know what you were downing, if not for the vibrant color. The recipe has been tweaked with the detoxifying goodness of chlorella, a micro-algae that supercharges the status of this smoothie to sky levels! Chlorella is also rich in chlorophyll and is a powerful supplement known to help strengthen the immune system.

Serves 2

Ingredients
Smoothie
½ cup unsweetened coconut milk
2 tablespoons chia seeds
½ small avocado
2 cups frozen peaches
1 ripe banana
Fresh ginger, 1" piece
2 pitted dates
1 cup spinach
1 teaspoon chlorella

Toppings
1 tablespoon coconut flakes
1 pinch cinnamon
1 banana, sliced
1 tablespoon cacao nibs
2 tablespoons blueberries and raspberries
1 tablespoon hemp seeds

Preparation
1. Blend all smoothie ingredients at high speed until smooth.
2. Transfer to a bowl and top with unsweetened coconut flakes, cinnamon, banana slices, cacao nibs, blueberries, raspberries and hemp seeds!

Nutrition facts per serving
Calories 397, carbs 41g, fats 27g, proteins 7g, sodium 24mg, sugars 23g.

Turmeric Avocado Banana Smoothie Bowl

This recipe proves how an exotic blend of ingredients creates something beautiful! While turmeric may be considered an Indian condiment, its miraculous health benefits have been advertised far and wide. What better way to kick-start your day with a meal packed to bursting with everything good that nature has to offer! Fight inflammation by adding this powerhouse to your smoothies and your mornings might just be brighter.

Serves 3

Ingredients
Smoothie
2 bananas, peeled and frozen
1 cup almond milk
2 tablespoons fresh turmeric
¼ ripe avocado
3 cups organic loose spinach
3 Medjool dates, pitted

Toppings
1 tablespoon shredded coconut
2 tablespoon flax seeds
1 blood orange, thinly sliced
1 granola bar, crumbled

Preparation
1. Toss all smoothie ingredients in to the blender and mix on high until the desired texture is achieved.
2. Top with shredded coconuts, Flax Seeds, blood oranges and Granola bars!

Nutrition facts per serving
Calories 548, carbs 56g, fats 35g, proteins 7g,
sodium 59mg, sugars 27g

Raspberry Mango Smoothie Bowl

Just the tempting name is enough to make one drool, but the creamy, gorgeously pink concoction is a pretty sight to behold.

Serves 2

Ingredients
Smoothie
1 banana
½ mango, frozen
½ avocado
1 cup raspberries
¼ cup coconut milk
⅔ cup coconut water
3 teaspoons chia seeds
1 tablespoon honey
2 tablespoons oats
2 tablespoons ground flax seeds

Toppings
3-4 strawberries, sliced
¼ cup raspberries

Preparation
1. Toss all smoothie ingredients in to the blender, except chia and flax seeds, and mix on high until a smooth puree forms.
2. Top with seeds of your fancy and slices of raspberry and strawberry.

Nutrition facts per serving
Calories 382, carbs 69g, fats 12g, proteins 8g, sodium 29mg, sugars 44g.

Avocado Persimmon Breakfast Bowl

Full of vigor and life, this rich and creamy smoothie provides a burst of omegas and invigorating energy! Avocados are packed with potassium, vitamins K, C, E and B, heart healthy mono-saturated fiber, and antioxidants, and help in regulating a normal blood pressure, promote healthy vision, help absorb nutrients from food and lower the blood cholesterol level! Combined with the goodness of persimmon, this smoothie is the ultimate dose of health!

Serves 1

Ingredients
Smoothie
1 persimmon (remove skin if not organic)
½ ripe avocado
2 tablespoons chia seeds
2 tablespoons pumpkin seeds
2 tablespoons almond butter (unsweetened)
1 tablespoon hemp protein powder
1 cup coconut water
1 teaspoon cinnamon
½ teaspoon nutmeg

Toppings
Sliced persimmon
Nutmeg seeds
Cinnamon

Preparation

1. Toss all the smoothie ingredients in to a blender and mix at medium speed. Slowly pour coconut water until a desired consistency is achieved.
2. Pour in a bowl and sprinkle the topping generously!

Nutrition facts per serving
Calories 605, carbs 42g, fats 37g, proteins 29g,
sodium 43mg, sugars 16g.

Raspberry Melon Baobab Smoothie

The height of summer is epitomized by luscious plump raspberries, succulent melons and the nutritious and fabulous citrus tang of baobab! This lip-smacking, detoxifying smoothie will rejuvenate your mood for the entire day, give you energy, ward off stress and fatigue, and besides, it's simply delectable to devour!

Serves 2

Ingredients
Smoothie
½ cup frozen raspberries
1 cup frozen cantaloupe chunks
1 cup unsweetened almond milk
1 scoop vanilla protein powder
1 teaspoon baobab powder
½ teaspoon psyllium husks
2 tablespoons peanut butter (crunchy or smooth, optional)
A few ice cubes

Toppings
2 tablespoons blueberries
2 tablespoons toasted shredded coconut
1 tablespoon cacao nibs

Preparation
1. Blend all the smoothie ingredients together, until a desired consistency is achieved.
2. Top with vibrant blueberries, coconut and cacao nibs and slurp. I mean eat!

Nutrition facts per serving
Calories 326, carbs 36g, fats 16g, proteins 19g,
sodium 220mg, sugars 12g

Carrot Cake Smoothie Bowl

Craving the indulgence of a decadently rich carrot cake, minus the calories and sugar, reminiscent of the warmth of winter? Rest assured, this smoothie bowl is a guilty (free) pleasure! Incorporating hemp seeds adds a dose of healthy fats and protein, while the bananas are perfect to render ample sweetness to the smoothie base. Plus, the tantalizing aroma of decadent spices truly makes this a passionate affair!

Serves 2

Ingredients
Smoothie
2 large bananas
1 large carrot, cut into pieces
1 scoop raw vanilla protein powder
¼ - ½ cup raw hemp milk or coconut milk
1 teaspoon pure vanilla extract
2 teaspoon cinnamon
½ teaspoon cardamom
¼ teaspoon nutmeg
Fresh ginger, 1" piece
Stevia to taste

Toppings
1 tablespoon goji berries
1 tablespoon raisins
1 tablespoon raw walnut pieces
1 tablespoon granulated bee pollen
1 tablespoon flaked dried coconut
1 tablespoon chia seeds
1 tablespoon ground flaxseed
1 tablespoon hemp seeds

Preparation:

1. Blend all the smoothie ingredients together, adding coconut milk until a desired consistency is achieved.
2. Transfer to a bowl, generously sprinkle toppings over the scrumptious delicacy and dig in!

Nutrition facts per serving
Calories 368, carbs 49g, fats 18g, proteins 15g, sodium 60mg, sugars 26g.

Mango Lucama Super-Green Smoothie

The super green smoothie is the ultimate health booster! Lucama powder is gluten-free and an abundant source of antioxidants, fiber, carbohydrates, vitamins, and minerals necessary for bodily functions and beneficial to the immune system. Even if you are not a fan of green, this smoothie is a great way to sneak some veggies into your diet without turning your nose up! Hallelujah!

Ingredients
Smoothie
1 cup soy milk
½ cup frozen mango
1 scoop vanilla protein powder (about 30g)
2 teaspoons lucama powder
½ teaspoon Spirulina powder
½ avocado
¼ cup kale leaves
¼ cup spinach
Few ice cubes

Toppings
½ kiwi, sliced
5 strawberries, sliced
1 tablespoon goji berries
1 tablespoon chia seeds
1 tablespoon cacao nibs

Preparation
1. Place all the smoothie ingredients in to the blender and rev it up until all the ingredients are thoroughly incorporated! You can add cold water if you want a thinner consistency.
2. Play with the toppings and turn your bowl into a piece of art!

Nutrition facts per serving
Calories 411, carbs 48g, fats 18g, proteins 20g, sodium 144mg, sugars 23g.

Chocolate Hazelnut Hemp Smoothie Bowl

Once you try a smoothie with decadent chocolate, you can never go back! While a chocolate smoothie might set off alarms in health buffs, incorporating hemp seeds packs the smoothie bowl with iron, omega-3 fats and plant based proteins! The slightly neutral taste of the hemp seeds is immaculately balanced by the sweetness of the bananas and chocolate.

Serves 1-2

Ingredients
Smoothie
2-3 frozen bananas
¼ cup hazelnuts, soaked 30 minutes
2 tablespoons hemp protein
2 tablespoons cacao powder
¾ cup unsweetened almond milk
3 Medjool dates, pitted

Toppings
1 banana, sliced
2 tablespoons hazelnuts, chopped
1 tablespoon cacao nibs
1 tablespoon hemp seeds

Preparation
1. Blend all the smoothie ingredients together, until a desired consistency is achieved.
2. Pour in to a bowl and embellish with mouth-watering crunchy toppings.
3. Serve cold!

Nutrition facts per serving
Calories 492, carbs 85g, fats 15g, proteins 14g,
sodium 69mg, sugars 51g.

Pineapple, Banana, and Peach Smoothie Bowl

It's hard not to be smitten with the explosive tropical punch of plump peaches and tangy pineapples in this refreshing smoothie! A quick glance at the gorgeous gem-like tones will make you smile every time! This definitely beats your standard oatmeal any day!

Serves 1

Ingredients

Smoothie
½ cup vanilla almond milk
¼ cup oats
1 cup pineapple, cut into chunks
1 peach, pitted
1 banana, frozen
1 small piece candied ginger
½ cup Greek yogurt

Toppings
2 tablespoons sunflower seeds
¼ cup blueberries
1 tablespoon honey
Peach slices

Preparation
1. Toss all the smoothie ingredients into the blender and mix on high speed, until a smooth puree is formed.
2. Transfer to a bowl and top generously with the scrumptious topping assortments.

Nutrition facts per serving
Calories 403, carbs 84g, fats 15g, proteins 16g, sodium 141mg, sugars 18g.

Berry Smoothie Bowl with Peach and Orange

The combination of fruity, crunchy and mega-vibrant smoothie will tantalize your taste buds and leave you feeling satiated, refreshed, and berry happy! Not only it is easy to whip up, but it serves to keep your body fueled all day long! One slurp and you could almost be greedy and devour the entire bowl yourself, and start your day sunny side up!

Serves 1

Ingredients
Smoothie
1 ½ cups frozen peaches
1 banana
½ cup orange juice, chilled (fresh squeezed, preferably)
½ cup blackberries
½ cup frozen blueberries

Toppings
¼ cup walnuts
2 tablespoon hemp seeds
Honey
2 tablespoons dried mulberries

Preparation
1. Blend all the smoothie ingredients until a rich ice cream consistency is achieved.
2. Transfer to a bowl and sprinkle with chopped walnuts, mulberries, hemp seeds and a drizzle of honey!

Nutrition facts per serving
Calories 674, carbs 103g, fats 20g, proteins 18g, sodium 50mg, sugars 74g.

Blueberry, Spinach, Pineapple Smoothie Bowl

The anti-oxidant rich blueberries, combined with the super powers of spinach, will leave your body singing hallelujah! With the intense signature taste and vibrant hue that only wild blueberries can impart, this fare is set to awe! This is what breakfast dreams are made of!

Serves 1-2

Ingredients

Smoothie
1 cup baby spinach leaves
1 cup blueberry
½ cup apple juice
½ cup ice
½ cup pineapple, chopped

Toppings
¼ cup puffed kamut cereal or puffed rice cereal
2 tablespoons pumpkin seeds
1 tablespoon flax seeds
½ cup blueberries
Honey

Preparation
1. Blend all the smoothie ingredients together, until a smooth consistency is achieved.
2. Pour in to a bowl and adorn with the crunchy toppings!
3. Serve cold and be ready for lip-smacking goodness!

Nutrition facts per serving
Calories 438, carbs 83g, fats 11g, proteins 9g, sodium 36mg, sugars 61g.

Peaches and Cream Smoothie Bowl

Give your morning smoothie a facelift with this pastel perfection! Creamy, rich, protein-filled, and peachy, textured with nutty crunchy oats, with a delicate vanilla aroma, this smoothie bowl is the perfect start to a day!

Serves 2

Ingredients

Smoothie
½ cup almond milk
1 teaspoon chia seeds
1 cup frozen peaches
1 frozen banana, chopped
1 tablespoon almond or cashew butter
1 teaspoon honey
½ teaspoon grated fresh ginger
½ teaspoon cinnamon

Toppings
1 peach, sliced
Fresh figs
1 tablespoon chopped pistachios
Mint sprigs
Oat crumble or granola

Preparation
1. Place all the smoothie ingredients into a blender and mix until thick and creamy.
2. Transfer to a bowl and garnish generously with thin slices of peaches and figs, with pistachios and oats, and throw in a sprig of mint for a smoothie that is almost too pretty to eat!

Nutrition facts per serving
Calories 497, carbs 56g, fats 28g, proteins 10g,
sodium 52mg, sugars 29g.

Dark Cherry Smoothie Bowl

Our bodies need fuel to survive the drudgery and relentless tasks of the day! The antioxidants and phytonutrients in cherries help fight free radicals, which may help reduce anxiety and depression and prove to be a mood booster. If that didn't convince you, the divine spoonful will!

Serves 1

Ingredients
Smoothie
2 cups frozen cherries, pitted
1 banana
¾ cup coconut water
2 scoops vanilla protein powder

Topping
8 whole cherries
¼ cup coconut flakes
¼ cup sliced almonds
¼ cup raw cacao nibs

Preparation
1. Blend all the smoothie ingredients, until a smooth lump-free consistency is formed.
2. Pour into a bowl and sprinkle with the gorgeously contrasting toppings to set off the exquisite red of the smoothie!
3. Grab a spoon and dig in (or slurp!).

Nutrition facts per serving
Calories 675, carbs 100g, fats 18g, proteins 29g, sodium 171mg, sugars 18g.

Blueberry Cacao Smoothie Bowl

The scrumptious smoothie is a textural paradise for your taste buds and the very face of happiness in a bowl! Adding plant-based protein powder would really help hold you over till your mid-morning snack attack!

Serves 2

Ingredients
Smoothie
1¼ cups unsweetened vanilla almond milk
1 cup frozen blueberries
1 cup frozen spinach
1 tablespoon cacao powder
1 tablespoon hemp seeds
2 Medjool dates
1 scoop vanilla brown rice protein
A few drops of vanilla extract

Toppings
1 tablespoon coconut flakes
2 tablespoons cacao nibs
2 tablespoons goji berries
2 tablespoons blueberries
1 granola bar, crumbled

Preparation
1. Blend all smoothie ingredients, until a smooth creamy puree is formed.
2. Transfer to a bowl and play with the toppings!

Nutrition facts per serving
Calories 333, carbs 47g, fats 9g, proteins 18g,
sodium 225mg, sugars 28g.

Blue Morning Smoothie Bowl

This smoothie bowl packs a surprise element; what makes this creamy luxurious breakfast fare blue is the nutrient bursting spirulina and not blueberries! If you are shrewdly keeping tabs on your carbohydrate or sugar intakes, this smoothie bowl should make the center of your table!

Serves 2

Ingredients
Smoothie
1 banana, frozen
1 large zucchini, frozen
½ cup low-fat coconut milk,
2 tablespoons chia seeds
2 tablespoons cashew butter
1 teaspoon organic spirulina, powdered
Pinch of sea salt
Dash of cinnamon

Toppings
1 tablespoon hemp seeds
2 tablespoons goji berries
1 bar pumpkin spiced granola
¼ cup blueberries
2 tablespoons coconut flakes

Preparation
1. Blend all the smoothie ingredients until a thick puree forms.
2. Transfer to a bowl and garnish with the beautiful toppings.
3. Serve immediately.

Nutrition facts per serving
Calories 459, carbs 49g, fats 9g, proteins 10g,
sodium 139mg, sugars 26g.

Sunrise Smoothie Bowl

The sweet zesty and refreshing smoothie bowl would instill a spring to your step all day! This Sunrise Smoothie Bowl is so vibrant and gorgeous; it will make you feel tremendously energized and cheery inside, while a little bit healthier; one spoonful at a time.

Serves 1-2

Ingredients
Smoothie
1 kiwi
1 banana – frozen chunks
1/3 cup orange juice, chilled
½ cup plain yogurt or Greek yogurt

Toppings
2 tablespoons chia seeds
4 tablespoons granola
2 tablespoons toasted coconut
1 tablespoon nuts
2 tablespoons mint
1 kiwi, sliced

Preparation
1. Slice kiwis in half and spoon the fruit out.
2. Toss all the smoothie ingredients in to the blender and blend until creamy and thick.
3. Pour in to a bowl and creatively place the toppings over the surface!

Nutrition facts per serving
Calories 588, carbs 94g, fats 30g, proteins 23g, sodium 88mg, sugars 46g

Chocolate Almond Butter Smoothie Bowl

Concocted with wholesome ingredients and the rich decadency of chocolate, this fare personifies a bona fide good-to-wake-up-to potion! As you are not constrained to slurping the bowl with a straw, be as ingenious with your toppings as your heart desires!

Serves 1

Ingredients
Smoothie
1 cup chocolate milk
2 bananas, frozen chunks
1 tablespoon dark cocoa powder
2 tablespoons almond butter

Toppings
1 banana, sliced
1 tablespoon almond flakes
1 tablespoon almond butter
1 tablespoon chia seeds
1 tablespoon hemp seeds

Preparation
1. Place all the smoothie ingredients into the blender.
2. Blend on low speed, slowly adding milk, until a thick puree is formed.
3. Pour in to a blender and intersperse desired toppings over the top.

Nutrition facts per serving
Calories 983, carbs 125g, fats 46g, proteins 28g,
sodium 154 mg, sugars 67g.

Pina-Colada Breakfast Smoothie

One slurp of the Aloha smoothie will transport you to the sunny tropics in a jiffy. Simply classic, irresistible and super easy to whip up! You might not be in paradise, but your mornings can be bright, just the same.

Serves 1

Ingredients

Smoothie
½ cup light coconut milk
1 banana, frozen chunks
1 cup pineapple, frozen chunks
½ tablespoon freshly squeezed lime juice

Toppings
¼ cup homemade granola
1 tablespoon hemp seeds
¼ cup fresh fruit, such as raspberries, strawberries, pineapple, mango, or blackberries
6 Hemp Heart Bites™ roughly chopped
1 tablespoon bee pollen
1 tablespoon mixed nuts

Preparation
1. Place all smoothie ingredients in a blender and blend until a smooth puree forms
2. Pour into a bowl and sprinkle toppings to embellish the hearty bowl!

Nutrition facts per serving
Calories 605, carbs 67g, fats 37g, proteins 11g,
sodium 49 mg, sugars 39g.

Choco Cherry Breakfast Smoothie Bowl

Incorporating a little creativity in your meals is always a good idea! The tartness of the cherries, complemented by the bitterness of the chocolate and balanced by the subtle sweetness imparted by the coconuts, is a commendable concoction; packed with vitamins, ultra powerful antioxidants, plant-based proteins and fiber and the love of an ever-lasting chocolate affair!

Serves 1-2

Ingredients
Smoothie
1½ cups cherries, frozen
1 6-ounce Greek yogurt
1 banana
½ -1 cup almond milk
¼ cup coconut, shredded

Toppings
1 tablespoon chia seeds
1 granola bar
1 banana, sliced
1 tablespoon chocolate chips
1 tablespoon pine nuts

Preparation
1. Blend all ingredients in the blender, slowly adding milk, until the desired consistency is achieved.
2. Pour in a bowl and generously add your toppings. Dig in!

Nutrition facts per serving
Calories 511, carbs 77g, fats 22g, proteins 18g, sodium 138 mg, sugars 47g.

Blueberry Cheesecake Smoothie Bowl

If you were to take a slice of your all-time favorite blueberry cheesecake and put it in the blender, it would taste exactly like this smoothie! Blueberries are the ultimate powerhouse when it comes to nutrients. They are packed with phytonutrients, antioxidants, vitamin C and K, and fiber, and we love to incorporate them in our breakfasts!

Serves 1

Ingredients
Smoothie
1 ½ cups blueberries
3 tablespoons honey
¼ cup cream cheese
½ cup milk
Handful ice cubes

Toppings
2 graham crackers, crushed
6-7 fresh blueberries
2 tablespoons cacao nibs

Preparation
1. Crush two graham crackers in the food processor and set aside.
2. Toss all the smoothie ingredients into the blender and blend on high for 2-3 minutes, until a thick consistency is achieved.
3. Pour into a bowl and top with crushed graham crackers, blueberries, and cacao nibs.

Nutrition facts per serving
Calories 658, carbs 147g, fats 19g, proteins 11g, sodium 281mg, sugars 91g.

Vegan Blackberry Coconut Smoothie

Coconut milk affords uncontested creaminess and decadence to any fare, and this delectable breakfast bowl is no exception! Beautifully contrasted by the ebony black of the berries, the smoothie provides the perfect kick-start to your mornings.

Serves 1

Ingredients
Smoothie
1 cup blackberries
1 ripe banana
1 cup coconut milk
½ cup spinach leaves

Toppings
2 teaspoons chia seeds
2 teaspoons raw pumpkin seeds
2 tablespoons coconut flakes
Fresh blackberries

Preparation
1. Blend together spinach, banana, and coconut milk, until a smooth puree forms.
2. Add blackberries and pulse a few times to incorporate.
3. Pour in to a bowl and sprinkle generously with toppings.

Nutrition facts per serving
Calories 539, carbs 39g, fats 44g, proteins 8g,
sodium 36mg, sugars 20g.

Banana Cream Pie Smoothie Bowl

The creamy vanilla base of this smoothie bowl is reminiscent of the banana cream pie — nobody can resist! If you happen to have some bananas handy, whip up this nutritious smoothie bowl and indulge in your sweet tooth!

Serves 1

Ingredients
Smoothie
3 bananas, frozen chunks
¼ - ½ cup coconut milk
1 tablespoon raw maca powder
1 tablespoon raw lucama powder
A few drops vanilla extract
Stevia to taste

Toppings
1 banana, sliced
1 tablespoon flaked dried coconut
1 tablespoon bee pollen
1 tablespoon cacao nibs
1 teaspoon ground flaxseed
1 teaspoon chia seeds
1 teaspoon hemp seeds

Preparation
1. Blend all the smoothie ingredients in the blender. Keep adding milk until a desired consistency is achieved.
2. Pour in a bowl and embellish with the crunchy toppings to imbue a contrasting texture to your breakfast bowl.

Nutrition facts per serving
Calories 439, carbs 83g, fats 12g, proteins 7g, sodium 10mg, sugars 42g.

Mango, Beet and Banana Smoothie Bowl

The beautiful amalgamation of three nutrition powerhouses is the ultimate soul food your body is asking for! Mango is rich in pre-biotic dietary fiber, vitamins, minerals, and poly-phenolic flavonoid antioxidant compounds. Combined with the iron-packed beet roots, this wondrous smoothie satiates your dietary needs for hours!

Serves 1

Ingredients
Smoothie
1 cup frozen mango
⅔ cup raw beets, cubed
1 banana, sliced
½ cup vanilla almond milk
2 dates, pitted

Toppings
2 tablespoons hemp seeds
¼ cup granola
Sliced fruit of your choice

Preparation
1. Toss all the smoothie ingredients into the blender and mix on high speed, until a smooth puree is formed.
2. Transfer to a bowl and top generously with an assortment of scrumptious toppings.

Nutrition facts per serving
Calories 591, carbs 136g, fats 26g, proteins 22g,
sodium 124mg, sugars 84g.

Vanilla Raspberry Smoothie

How would you like to guzzle down an ice cream sundae for breakfast, without putting on the pounds, and yet incorporating heaps of nutrition in your body? No, it is not wishful thinking because this smoothie bowl does exactly that!

Serves 2

Ingredients

Smoothie
1 banana, frozen
1 cup raspberries, frozen
1 cup almond milk
2 scoops vanilla protein powder
2 tablespoons chia seeds
2 tablespoons water

Toppings
¼ cup granola
Fresh raspberries
2 tablespoons cacao nibs

Preparation
1. Combine all smoothie ingredients in a blender and blend at high speed until a thick puree forms.
2. Pour in a bowl, top with the crumbles of your favorite granola bar, and dive in!

Nutrition facts per serving
Calories 852, carbs 75g, fats 48g, proteins 38g, sodium 150mg, sugars 17g.

Strawberry Cheesecake Smoothie Bowl

The bane of every health buff is the love of strawberry cheesecake conflicting with the calorie curbing resolutions! However, this amazingly delicious smoothie bowl will give you all the scrumptiousness of a hearty slice of strawberry cheesecake, complemented with heaps of nutrition; the strawberries are packed with fiber and vitamins, while the Greek yogurt chips in a healthy dose of protein!

Serves 1

Ingredients

Smoothie
½ cup strawberries
½ cup Greek yogurt
1 tablespoon cream cheese
¼ cup almond milk
Few drops of vanilla extract
Ice cubes

Toppings
1 teaspoon chia seeds
2 graham crackers, roughly chopped
2 tablespoons almonds

Preparation
1. Toss all the ingredients for the smoothie in to the blender and blend on low speed until thick and creamy.
2. Pour into a bowl and festoon with the mouth-watering toppings!

Nutrition facts per serving
Calories 451, carbs 48g, fats 23g, proteins 27g, sodium 253mg, sugars 18g.

Mango Ginger Good-Eats Bowl

If you are feeling the mango kick this summer, this smoothie is just the one for you, while the ginger adds an energizing zing to the bowl and is perfect for an early morning kick start.

Serves 1

Ingredients
Smoothie
1 mango, chopped
2 bananas, frozen
2 tablespoons coconut yogurt
1 tablespoon peanut butter (smooth)
1 knob ginger
2 dates, pitted

Topping
1 tablespoon coconut flakes
1 tablespoon chia seeds
1 buckwheat granola bar
¼ cup chopped fruit; mango, berries, figs

Preparation
1. Blend all smoothie ingredients together at medium speed, until a smooth puree forms.
2. Top with the delectable topping options and enjoy!

Nutrition facts per serving
Calories 612, carbs 125g, fats 13g, proteins 10g, sodium 83mg, sugars 87g.

Peanut Butter Berry Acai Bowl

Whipped in to exquisite smoothies, pressed in to juices or sprinkled over a bowl of cereal, acai berries are a versatile treat!

Serves 2

Ingredients
Smoothie
1 acai smoothie pack
1 cup coconut water
1 cup frozen strawberries
1 cup frozen mixed berries
2 tablespoons peanut butter

Toppings
1 tablespoon flax seeds
1 tablespoon chia seeds
1 tablespoon goji berries
1 tablespoon cacao nibs
2 tablespoons fresh berries
1 tablespoon hemp seeds

Preparation
1. Toss in all the smoothie ingredients into the blender and mix at medium speed.
2. Pour out when an ice cream consistency is reached.
3. Sprinkle the toppings generously and indulge in your sweet tooth with this heartily satisfying (but not too heavy) smoothie!

Nutrition facts per serving
Calories 816, carbs 88g, fats 40g, proteins 22g, sodium 235mg, sugars 48g.

Chocolate-Mint Green Smoothie Bowl

Thick, creamy, chocolaty and tastes like an after eight- what's not to love about this delicious smoothie bowl! The mint-chocolate flavor of the smoothie is imbued by the pepper mint extract and the decadent cacao nibs, while kale and avocado incorporate healthy fibers and antioxidants to the fare!

Serves 1

Ingredients
Smoothie
1½ cups non-dairy milk
4 kale leaves
½ avocado
1 teaspoon peppermint extract
1½ - 2 tablespoons cacao powder
1 scoop chocolate protein powder
Sprig of mint

Toppings
1 tablespoon cacao nibs
1 tablespoon coconut flakes
1 banana, sliced

Preparation
1. Combine all smoothie ingredients in a blender, and pulse until smooth.
2. Pour in to a bowl and top with a smatter over the toppings, and dig in to the big bowl of heaven!

Nutrition facts per serving
Calories 538, carbs 60g, fats 30g, proteins 19g, sodium 78mg, sugars 16g.

Enlighten Smoothie Bowl

A fruity rainbow bowl, packed full of antioxidants, vitamins, and super foods, this smoothie is the ultimate decadent vegan dessert! Since fruits cannot fulfill the protein requirement of the body, a vegan protein powder is incorporated in the bowl.

Serves 1

Ingredients
Smoothie
1 ½ cups frozen berry mix
1 ½ fresh banana
1 scoop vegan protein powder
½ cup almond milk
3 – 4 ice cubes

Toppings
1 bar granola, crumbled
1 tablespoon cacao nibs
1 tablespoon natural nut butters (almond, peanut, etc.)
1 banana, sliced
1 tablespoon blueberries
1 tablespoon hemp hearts
1 teaspoon chia seed

Preparation
1. Blend all the smoothie ingredients in a blender, until a thick and creamy consistency is reached.
2. Pour in a bowl and top with all the delicious toppings.

Nutrition facts per serving
Calories 971, carbs 138g, fats 41g, proteins 38g, sodium 278mg, sugars 74g.

Muesli Greek Yogurt Smoothie Bowl

Muesli is one of the healthiest breakfast options, incorporating whole grains, antioxidants, and high fiber which aids in digestion and keeps you feeling satiated for a long time! Plus, the berry-licious smoothie is simply a delight to devour! This is what breakfast dreams are made of!

Serves 2

Ingredients
Smoothie
1 cup frozen strawberries
1 banana
1 cup Greek 100 vanilla yogurt

Toppings
½ cup fresh mixed berries
½ cup toasted oats muesli
1 tablespoon chia seeds

Preparation
1. Blend together all the smoothie ingredients, until a smooth puree forms.
2. Pour in to a bowl, top with muesli and fresh berries and serve!

Nutrition facts per serving
Calories 310, carbs 51g, fats 49g, proteins 15g, sodium 107mg, sugars 23g.

Cherry Berry Smoothie Bowl

This smoothie rendition incorporates the brilliant red summer essence of cherries, the sweetness of ripe bananas, the subtle tang of berries, and the tantalizing aroma of vanilla, to concoct a sorbet-like dessert for a reprieve in the sweltering heat!

Serves 3

Ingredients
Smoothie
1 ripe banana, frozen
2 cups frozen pitted cherries
1 ¼ cups low-fat milk (1%)
½ tsp vanilla extract

Toppings
¼ cup shredded dried unsweetened coconut
1 tablespoon chia seeds
¼ cup sliced almonds
½ cup fresh blueberries
½ cup fresh raspberries

Preparation
1. Blend together all the smoothie ingredients, until a smooth puree is formed.
2. Divide in to individual bowls and top with berries, crunchy almonds and chia seeds! Enjoy.

Nutrition facts per serving
Calories 210, carbs 32 g, fats 8 g, proteins 6 g, sodium 35 mg, sugars 21 g.

Chai Infused Chia Smoothie Bowl

Chock full of powerful anti-inflammatory, antiviral, and antioxidant agents, this fall-inspired smoothie bowl, steeped with the enticing aroma of chai, will leave you feeling nourished and contented from inside out!

Serves 1

Ingredients
Smoothie
2 cups almond milk
1 scoop vanilla protein powder (optional)
2 chai tea bags
1-2 teaspoons turmeric
½ teaspoon cinnamon powder
1 tablespoon honey
2 tablespoons chia seeds
1 tablespoon almond butter
2 bananas, frozen
1 cup ice

Toppings
1 tablespoon chia seeds
1 tablespoon hemp seeds
1 banana, sliced

Preparation
1. Steep the chai teabags in hot milk, with turmeric and cinnamon, for 5 minutes.
2. Remove tea bag and add the milk to the blender with the remaining smoothie ingredients.
3. Blend until a smooth puree forms.
4. Pour in to a bowl and have fun with the toppings!

Nutrition facts per serving
Calories 811, carbs 66g, fats 29g, proteins 36g,
sodium 748mg, sugars 38g.

Cherry Apple Smoothie Fare

This scrumptious, healthy bowl is a combination of fresh local goodness and super foods, served beautifully in a chilled vibrant serving!

Serves 1-2

Ingredients
Smoothie
1 cup cherries
1 cup frozen organic mixed berries (cranberries and blueberries)
1 tart summer apple
1 scoop vegan protein powder
½ cup water

Topping
2 tablespoons mixed berries
1 tablespoon chia seeds
1 tablespoon unsweetened coconut

Preparation
1. Blend all the smoothie ingredients in the blender, slowing adding splashes of water until the desired consistency is achieved.
2. Pour in a bowl and garnish with the toppings before serving.

Nutrition facts per serving
Calories 353, carbs 62g, fats 5.g, proteins 14g, sodium 113mg, sugars 15g.

Banana Split Smoothie Bowl

The classic banana split is a real crowd pleaser and quintessential (guilty pleasure) dessert. Here's how you can concoct a rendition with double the flavor and half the calories!

Serves 2

Ingredients
Smoothie
¾ cup milk or coconut milk
2 ripe bananas, frozen chunks
1 scoop of protein powder
½ cup fresh strawberries, sliced

Toppings
1 fresh banana, sliced
½ cup fresh pineapple, diced
1 teaspoon chia seeds
2 tablespoon sliced almonds
1/8 cup dark chocolate chips
2 maraschino cherries
A dollop of whipping cream or low-fat yogurt

Preparation
1. Blend all the smoothie ingredients until a thick puree forms.
2. Pour into chilled bowls and top with banana and pineapple slices, sprinkle chia seeds, almond flakes and chocolate chips generously, drop a dollop of whipping cream and top up with a cherry!

Nutrition facts per serving
Calories 435, carbs 63g, fats 13g, proteins 16g,
sodium 93mg, sugars 38g.

Grapefruit Smoothie Bowl

Up your smoothie game a notch with the pinky deliciousness of grapefruit and this fruity crunchy bowl is everything that a breakfast should be! The bitterness of the grapefruit is offset by the maple syrup and bananas and even the non-grapefruit-lovers are bound to be smitten by this fare!

Serves 2

Ingredients
Smoothie
½ grapefruit
1 banana
8 strawberries
¼ cup oats
3 tablespoons organic maple syrup
4 ice cubes
¼ cup cashews
Mint sprig
¼ cup pink grapefruit juice

Toppings
2 tablespoons pineapple chunks
1 tablespoon coconut flakes
4 strawberries
1 tablespoon hemp seeds
1 tablespoon chia seeds

Preparation
1. Blend all the smoothie ingredients in the blender, until a smooth puree forms.
2. Pour in a bowl, top with the scrumptious toppings and dig in!

Nutrition facts per serving
Calories 438, carbs 804g, fats 13g, proteins 8g, sodium 22mg, sugars 58g.

Chocolate Tahini Dates Smoothie Bowl

If you happen to love a hearty fulfilling breakfast, this thick, creamy and decadent smoothie perfectly fits the bill!

Serves 2

Ingredients
Smoothie
1 banana, frozen chunks
2 tablespoons tahini
3 Medjool dates
1 tablespoon raw cacao powder
1 teaspoon vanilla extract
½ teaspoon ground cinnamon
¾ cup unsweetened almond milk

Toppings
1 tablespoon sesame seeds
1 tablespoon cacao nibs
1 tablespoon goji berries
1 tablespoon slivered almonds

Preparation
1. Place all the smoothie ingredients in to the blender and whirl away until a smooth consistency is achieved.
2. Pour in to a bowl, top with the lovely toppings and enjoy!

Nutrition facts per serving
Calories 439, carbs 77g, fats 15g, proteins 8g, sodium 101mg, sugars 55g

Butternut Molasses Smoothie Bowl

Butternut and molasses are an underrated match made in heaven! The smoothie is loaded with superfood nutrition to keep you satiated for hours and the addition of molasses imbue a burst of iron in to the delectable spread!

Serves 2

Ingredients
Smoothie
1 ½ cups unsweetened almond milk
½ cup cooked butternut squash, pureed
1 banana, frozen
1 tablespoon chia seeds
1-2 tablespoons almond butter
½ tablespoon blackstrap molasses
3 Medjool dates, pitted
1 teaspoon pure vanilla extract
1 teaspoon ground cinnamon
¼ teaspoon ground nutmeg
¼ teaspoon ground ginger

Toppings
1 tablespoon cacao nibs
1 tablespoon pecans
1 tablespoon pumpkin seeds
1 tablespoon hemp seeds
Drizzle of pure maple syrup

Preparation
1. Chop and soak the Medjool dates in water for about 5 minutes, until soft.
2. Blend all the smoothie ingredients in blender, until a smooth puree forms.

3. Pour in a chilled bowl, top with your favorite goodies, drizzle over some maple syrup and enjoy!

Nutrition facts per serving
Calories 465, carbs 63g, fats 22g, proteins 11g, sodium 139mg, sugars 37g.

Probiotic Kefir Smoothie Bowl

The tart and refreshing essence of kefir resembles that of the yogurt but the naturally occurring bacteria and yeast in kefir supplies additional health benefits. It is loaded with valuable vitamins and minerals and contains easily digestible complete proteins.

Serves 1

Ingredients
Smoothie
1 cup Lifeway Plain Low Fat Kefir™
2 bananas, frozen
¼ cup almond or peanut butter

Toppings
1 tablespoon almonds
1 tablespoon raw honey
1 tablespoon bee pollen
1 tablespoon unsweetened shredded coconut
1 teaspoon dark chocolate chips
1 tablespoon chia seeds
1 tablespoon berries
1 banana, sliced

Preparation
1. Toss all the smoothie ingredients in to a bowl and whirl on medium speed until a desired consistency is achieved.
2. Pour in to a bowl and top with your favorite toppings.

Nutrition facts per serving
Calories 539, carbs 66g, fats 25g, proteins 17g, sodium 90mg, sugars 37g

Vanilla Almond Smoothie Bowl

This smoothie is a delectable milkshake in disguise and one that you will absolutely love!

Serves 1

Ingredients
Smoothie
2 cups low fat milk
2 scoops natural vanilla protein powder
2 tablespoons toasted slivered almonds
1 banana
3-4 ice cubes

Toppings
1 banana, sliced
1 tablespoon almonds
1 tablespoon unsweetened coconut
1 tablespoon chia seeds

Preparation
1. Place all the smoothie ingredients in to the blender, and blend until a thick ice cream consistency is achieved.
2. Transfer to a bowl and garnish creatively with the toppings.
3. Serve chilled.

Nutrition facts per serving
Calories 833, carbs 100g, fats 22g, proteins 68g, sodium 486mg, sugars 72g

More Books by Sarah Spencer

Here are some of Sarah Spencer's other cookbooks.

SIMPLE
PALEO
SALAD
COOKBOOK
50 QUICK & EASY
GLUTEN-FREE SALAD RECIPES
FEEL ENERGIZED, LOSE WEIGHT
AND LOOK HEALTHY
SARAH SPENCER

DELICIOUS
200-CALORIE
DESSERT
RECIPES
Perfect for Your Sweet Tooth
and Waistline!
SARAH SPENCER

NO SUGAR ADDED
HEALTHY
FROZEN
DESSERT
Recipes
Ice Pop, Slush, Sorbet, Treat on Stick, Frozen Yogurt,
Frozen drink, Pie, Bar, Parfait and More
LOUISE DAVIDSON

Appendix - Cooking Conversion Charts

1. Measuring Equivalent Chart

Type	Imperial	Imperial	Metric
Weight	1 dry ounce		28g
	1 pound	16 dry ounces	0.45 kg
Volume	1 teaspoon		5 ml
	1 dessert spoon	2 teaspoons	10 ml
	1 tablespoon	3 teaspoons	15 ml
	1 Australian tablespoon	4 teaspoons	20 ml
	1 fluid ounce	2 tablespoons	30 ml
	1 cup	16 tablespoons	240 ml
	1 cup	8 fluid ounces	240 ml
	1 pint	2 cups	470 ml
	1 quart	2 pints	0.95 l
	1 gallon	4 quarts	3.8 l
Length	1 inch		2.54 cm

* Numbers are rounded to the closest equivalent

2. Oven Temperature Equivalent Chart

T(°F)	T(°C)
220	100
225	110
250	120
275	140
300	150
325	160
350	180
375	190
400	200
425	220
450	230
475	250
500	260

* T(°C) = [T(°F)-32] * 5/9

** T(°F) = T(°C) * 9/5 + 32

*** Numbers are rounded to the closest equivalent

Printed in Great Britain
by Amazon